The Most Difficult Choices You'll N[...]

Would you rather. . .

be able to simulate the voice of anybody you meet *OR* simulate the hair?

Would you rather. . .

never be able to experience orgasm *OR* perpetually experience orgasm?

Would you rather. . .

have worms for eyelashes *OR* corduroy skin?

Would You Rather...? 2
E L E C T R I C   B O O G A L O O

Over **300** More **Absolutely Absurd Dilemmas** to Ponder

Second Edition

Justin Heimberg & David Gomberg

Published by Falls Media
1 Astor Place Penthouse K
New York, NY 10003

First Printing, 2nd Edition, November 2004
10   9   8   7   6   5   4   3   2
Printed in Canada
Design by Tom Schirtz

ISBN 0-9740439-3-1

Books are available at quantity discounts at www.wouldyourather.com
E-mail – info@wouldyourather.com

Acknowledgments

First and foremost, we'd like to thank our mothers who've made this and all things possible. Thanks also to our friends and families; half of our jokes were tested on them, and the other half were stolen from them. Thanks to Jay Mandel at the William Morris agency for his continuous help, guidance, and use of the word "hipster." And thanks to Sophia for being 100% pure petootie.

We'd like to recognize the contributions and help of: Jeff Sank, Jason Heimberg, Paul Katz, Todd DeHart, Matt Scharf, Dave Miller, Jonah Van Zandt, Dan Binstock, Bob Bernstein, Kert (with an "e") Mease, Todd Wagnon, Darren A. LaVerne, Grimaldi, Boesch, Eric Gomberg, Nicky Siegel, Brian "Sugar Daddy" Sugar, Dan "The Man" Levitan, Jon Mirsky, Aaron Hilliard, Kit Pongetti, Charlie Kranz, Steve Harwood, and Joliene Hamodot (the smartest woman in the world).

About the authors

Justin Heimberg   David Gomberg

Would you rather be...

Justin Heimberg, an idealistic comedy writer with a consistent outside jumper, who poses for photographs with an artificially forlorn look in his eyes

OR

David Gomberg, a vegetarian Internet baron with reasonable low-post moves, whose gleaming smile belies severe existential angst and inner turmoil?

Things to consider: Justin has done and continues to do things, some of which he receives money for. These things include writing movies, books, creating games and working with DreamYard/LA, an arts education non-profit that works with at-risk youth in Los Angeles. He recently returned to live in his home town near Washington DC. David Gomberg was born in one of Earth's alternate futures of the 31st Century (a different one from that which was conquered by the alien Badoon) and being a man of adventure in a time of world peace and prosperity, he was discontent. Discovering the parts of a time machine and the plans for its assembly in the ruins of one of his ancestors' property, the man who would become Gomberg embarked upon a life of conquest and adventure, exploring and ransacking time era after time era, under such guises as Pharaoh Rama-Tut, Kang the Conqueror, and others. He established strongholds or kingdoms across time. By his constant time travel, he diverged countless temporal counterparts to himself, each capable of independent existence and further travel.

CHECK OUT OUR WEBSITE AT WWW.WOULDYOURATHER.COM

Other Books by Justin Heimberg and David Gomberg:

Would You Rather...? by Justin Heimberg and David Gomberg

Do Unto Others by Justin Heimberg and David Gomberg

The World's Worst Book by Justin Heimberg

The Official Movie Plot Generator by the Brothers Heimberg

This is a book I do not show my rabbi.
                                        -David Gomberg

About The Deity

The ringmaster/MC/overlord of the *Would You Rather...* empire is "the deity." Visually and psychologically a cross between Charles Manson and Gabe Kaplan, the deity is the one responsible for creating and presenting the *WYR* dilemmas. It is the deity who asks "Would you rather...watch a porno movie with your parents or a porno movie starring your parents?" And it is the deity who orders, without exception, that you must choose. No one knows exactly why he does this; suffice to say, it's for reasons beyond your understanding. The deity communicates with you not through speech, nor telepathy, but rather through several sharp blows to the stomach that vary in power and location. Nearly omnipotent, often ruthless, and obsessed with former NBA seven-footers, the deity is a random idea generator with a peculiar predilection for intervening in your life in the strangest ways.

Contents

A Note from the Authors

Keepin' It Surreal

Would You Rather...? has been called many things: "Salvador Dali meets Mad Magazine"; "Fyodor Dostoevsky Meets Terrance Trent D'arby"; "Justin Heimberg Meets David Gomberg." Some have labeled it "a remarkable feat of post-structuralism"; others have deemed it "156 pages of sugar-coated anti-midget propaganda." It's been praised as "endless fun and surprisingly thought-provoking"; and lamented as a "crusade to end literature" and "too Judy Tenutaesque." One thing's for sure, for better or for worse, *WYR* has made its mark on the Free World.

Its success spawned numerous rip-offs and emulations: *This or That, Choose or Die, Which Do You Prefer?* and *Wouldn't You Rather...: Over Two Hundred Absolutely Absurd Pointed Questions to Ponder.* Out came the calendars, greeting cards, and lunch boxes. Next followed shirts, posters, pants, pins, pens, dioramas, action figures, sweat suits, catalytic converters, an after school special, and the world famous *Would you rather... Fly Girls*. As we speak, there are plans for a *WYR* movie, and tales circulate that the part of Miguel will go to Bruce Willis.

Of course, once every merchandising angle had been exhausted, we were forced to actually come up with some new material. We experimented with other easy-to-write gimmick/catch-phrase books.

If I Conquered France, I'd...
You Know Who Would Look Good In Jerry Curls is...
You Know You Have an Effective Catch-phrase When...
Do You Look Like a Pharaoh?
Barbara Mikulski Would Be More Popular If...
Aluminum Socks: The Guide to Making Your Own Clothing
It Hurts When I...

These titles, while promising, never quite came together, and we realized it would be easiest to publish another *Would You Rather...?* book. So was born: *Would You Rather 2: Electric Boogaloo.*

This was five years ago. The original *WYR2* was packaged in a neon jaundice cover and left to rest in peace in its vertical grave between the works of Lewis Grizzard and Cynthia Heimel. Until Now!!!

WYR 2 has been raised from the dead, repackaged, re-edited, amended, expanded, dissected, reassembled and distilled into a more perfect sequel. References that are no longer topical have been replaced, and obscure anti-icons who are now too popular have been replaced by less topical references. The result: *Would You Rather...? 2... uh... 2.*

How to use this book

Sit around with a bunch of friends and read a question to each other, discussing it until the momentum of the conversation fades into awkward silence and nervous glances. Everybody must choose. As the deity proclaims, YOU MUST CHOOSE! That's the whole premise of this thing. It forces you to really think about the options. Once everyone has chosen, move on to the next question. It's that simple. We have provided a few things to consider when deliberating each question, but don't restrict yourself to these, as much of the fun comes from imagining the different ways your choice will affect your life.

Whether played with friends or used as bathroom literary fodder, (or both if you have an extremely open and intimate circle of friends) *Would You Rather...?* will make you laugh, make you think, and make you very confused. So turn the page, read on, and embarrass yourself by mumbling in public "I could have done this. Damnit, why didn't I think of this? I could have made so much money. Damnit!"

CHAPTER 1

CURSED AGAIN!

These are the circumstances. An all too familiar deity descends from on high and informs you that, for reasons beyond your understanding, you must live the remainder of you life plagued with a terrible curse— an outrageous physical deformity, a bizarre behavioral disorder, an irksome inconvenience, etc. You need not feel entirely power-less, however. He allows you to choose between two possible fates.

Would you rather...

make the sounds of the bionic man when straining physically

OR

make the sound of the *Jeopardy* theme when straining mentally?

Things to consider: test-taking, gym class

Would you rather...

be compelled to enter every room by jumping into the doorway with an imaginary pistol drawn like the star of a 70's cop show

OR

invariably make your orgasm face instead of smiling when being photographed?

YOU MUST CHOOSE!

Would you rather be a Siamese twin...

connected at the soles of your feet *OR* at the lips?

by the finger tips *OR* by the hair?

at the buttocks *OR* at the elbows/knees?

your feet on your twin's shoulders *OR* his/her feet on yours?

with Joey Lawrence *OR* Kareem Abdul-Jabbar?

YOU MUST CHOOSE!

Would you rather...

have fingernails that grow at a rate of one inch per minute

OR

have pubic hair that grows at the same rate?

Things to consider: putting in contact lenses, sex life, tanning at the beach

Would you rather...

have Pamela Anderson's body from the waist up and Nel Carter's from the waist down

OR

Nel Carter's from the waist up and Pamela Anderson's from the waist down?

Things to consider: TV anchor career, toppling

YOU MUST CHOOSE!

Would you rather...

have bacon bit dandruff

OR

have the voice in your head sound like Jimmy Stewart?

YOU MUST CHOOSE!

Would you rather...

have lit candle wicks for hair *OR* asparagus for fingers?

worms for eyelashes *OR* corduroy skin?

carbonated blood *OR* leather fingernails?

Would you rather...

have glow-in-the-dark veins

OR

be able to watch only one television show for the rest of your life: *Charles in Charge* starring Scott Baio?

YOU MUST CHOOSE!

Would you rather...

have a nose that pulsates like a human heart

OR

be allowed to use only toothpaste for all hygiene purposes/processes?

Would you rather...

cough the sound of bagpipes

OR

fart the sound of chimes?

YOU MUST CHOOSE!

Would you rather...

have a comic book-style thought bubble

OR

a comic book-style dialogue bubble?

Things to consider: loss of privacy, hiding your thoughts with a big hat, ability to converse with the deaf, inability to converse with the blind, Why did that show *It's Your Move* go off the air so fast? How much credibility would John Kerry lose if he wore his hair in Jerry Curls?

YOU MUST CHOOSE!

Would you rather...

have a written lisp

OR

fizz up like Alkaseltzer when in the water?

Things to consider: thwimming

YOU MUST CHOOSE!

Would you rather...

have 14 navels OR 24 toes?

6 lips OR 34 fingers?

1 nostril OR 8 nostrils?

17 testicles OR 1 extremely restless one?

Things to consider: misshapen underwear

YOU MUST CHOOSE!

Would you rather...

speak to the tune of Village People songs

OR

have your sole means of locomotion be breakdancing?

Things to consider: What's the past tense of breakdance? Brokedance? Breakdanced?

YOU MUST CHOOSE!

Would you rather...

have invisible skin

OR

see in strobe light?

Things to consider: evening commute, modeling for biology text books

Would you rather...

have an intense urge to whisper sweet nothings into the ears of bus drivers as you pay your fare

OR

have parents who affectionately refer to you as "anal cakes"?

Things to consider: teacher-parent conferences, wedding toasts

YOU MUST CHOOSE!

Would you rather always have to wear...

pants four sizes too small *OR* ten-inch high heels?

a color combination of lavender and brown *OR* used **tea bag** earrings?

acid wash jeans *OR* **the male perm**?

hot pants *OR* a parrot?

NBA shorts circa 1979 *OR* an NBA hairstyle circa 1979?

Miller's outfits from ninth grade *OR* DeSena's outfits now?

Things to consider: **boldface** = good band name

YOU MUST CHOOSE!

Would you rather...

have permanent Cheetoh residue on your fingertips

OR

have skin that doesn't tan in the sun, but rather plaids?

Would you rather...

have anti-gravity hair

OR

have all your dreams written and directed by those guys who made those blaxploitation films of the 70's?

YOU MUST CHOOSE!

Hostage Crisis

These are the circumstances: You have been taken hostage by a group of militant terrorists (They work for the deity). The terrorists' leader says he will allow the US government to send one person in to negotiate your fate.

Would you rather your hostage negotiator be...

Dick Vitale *OR* Ike Turner?

Ozzy Osbourne *OR* Jessica Simpson?

Bobcat Goldthwait *OR* Marcel Marceau?

Jimmy Carter *OR* Pamela Anderson?

Charles Grodin *OR* "The American Dream" Dusty Rhodes?

YOU MUST CHOOSE!

Interior Motives

The deity is into Anti-Feng-Shui, the ancient Japanese art of the disharmonious placement and arrangement of objects in a given space. With this in mind, he decides your home needs some shaping up.

Would you rather...

have American cheese linens

OR

wall to wall ground beef carpet?

Would you rather...

Prince Valiant comic strip wallpaper

OR

Willis Reed permanently residing on your loveseat?

YOU MUST CHOOSE!

CHAPTER 2

MORE SEX

Like the deities and demi-gods of the Greeks, this is a godthing concerned with the earthly delights of hedonism. Perhaps "concerned" is not a strong enough word. Obsessed. Morbidly. Particularly in the comings and goings of his pet mortals. And so, for these reasons, and others beyond your understanding, he feels that your sex life could be so much more interesting.

Would you rather...

have your genitalia located on the top of your head

OR

the bottom of your left foot?

Things to consider: jogging, hats, the sexual act, masturbation

Would you rather...

have a permanent smile

OR

a permanent erection?

Things to consider: church, visiting grandma, funerals

YOU MUST CHOOSE!

Would you rather...

have genitalia that reduces in size two percent each time it is used

OR

genitalia that increases in twenty-five percent each time it is used?

Would you rather...

have your range of sexual body movement equal to that of a He-Man doll

OR

speak like Yoda when attracted to someone?

YOU MUST CHOOSE!

19

Would you rather...

have to call your parents and ask for permission every time you have sex

OR

be mandated to perform all sexual activity to Denise Williams' "Let's Hear it for the Boy"?

YOU MUST CHOOSE!

Would you rather have sex with...

Hillary Clinton *OR* Natalie from *Facts of Life?*

Oprah *OR* Rosie?

Daisy Duke in her prime *OR* Daphne from *Scooby Doo?*

Connie Chung *OR* a 200% enlarged Halle Berry?

Venus Williams *OR* Sheryl Crow if she spoke in the voice of an old Jewish man?

A "10" *OR* five "2's"? (At the same time)? A 10 *OR* two 4's and a 1? A 10 *OR* three 3.3's?

YOU MUST CHOOSE!

Would you rather have sex with...

Bryant Gumble *OR* "Weird" Al Yankovic?

Alex Trebec *OR* Larry David?

Yao Ming *OR* Mini-me from *Austin Powers*?

Johnny Depp without a leg *OR* Tom Selleck without a moustache?

Matt Damon *OR* Ben Affleck?

Matt Damon *OR* Ben Affleck if they exchanged heights?

YOU MUST CHOOSE!

During sex, would you rather...

utter all exclamations in the computerized voice of Stephen Hawking

OR

compulsively compliment yourself?

Would you rather...

be able to have sex exclusively with palindromes

OR

only be able to masturbate to the two wise-ass critics in the *Muppet Show?*

Things to consider: Lil, Anna, Otto, race car

YOU MUST CHOOSE!

Would you rather have sex with...

Meg Ryan and lose your sense of smell

OR

Janet Reno and earn the official title of "Commandant"?

Would you rather have sex with...

Matthew McConnohangy and lose a finger

OR

Burt Reynolds and learn how to properly spell "McConaughey"?

YOU MUST CHOOSE!

Would you rather...

never be able to experience orgasm

OR

perpetually experience orgasm?

Things to consider: life at the office, bar-mitzvahs, special pants, porn career

Would you...

dry hump Leonard Nimoy to gain complete knowledge of the "V" encyclopedia?

Things to consider: Vermont, Vatican City, Vulcans

YOU MUST CHOOSE!

The deity has always been one to fuel sibling rivalry.

Would you rather have sex with...

Alec *OR* Billy Baldwin?

Fred *OR* Ben Savage?

Orville *OR* Wilbur Wright?

Things to consider: Wilbur was hung like a Shetland pony.

YOU MUST CHOOSE!

Would you rather...

have a lover who is 6' tall with a 2 inch penis

OR

4' tall with a 12 inch penis? 3'tall with a 16 inch penis? 2' tall with a 26 inch penis?

YOU MUST CHOOSE!

Would you rather have a lover with measurements...

36-26-36 OR 33-23-34?

44-28-40 OR 34-18-30?

36-52-27 OR 54-8-26?

8-66-84 OR 114-75-12?

100-100-100 OR 36-24-36-26-58?

5-286-3 OR 38-26-44 (not necessarily in that order; measurements constantly shift)

YOU MUST CHOOSE!

Would you rather...

have Angelina Jolie as your personal sex slave

OR

an unlimited supply of pork? Jolie as your sex slave *OR* unlimited pork and season tickets to all sporting events? Jolie as your sex slave *OR* the pork, season tickets, and a personal minstrel who records your deeds in song?

YOU MUST CHOOSE!

Would you rather...

have joy buzzers built into your breasts

OR

have your g-spot located under your right armpit? In your left nostril? In the lunch box of a fifth grader in Milwaukee, Wisconsin?

YOU MUST CHOOSE!

Would you rather...

have an intense spot light perpetually shining from your crotch

OR

have your partner appear as Mao Tse-tung during sex?

Things to consider: receiving oral sex

YOU MUST CHOOSE!

Would you rather have sex with...

A 60% scale Jennifer Aniston *OR* a winged Kate Hudson?

Meryl Streep *OR* a severely jaundiced Britney Spears?

A profusely sweating Deborah Norville *OR* a butter-soaked Margot Kidder?

A three way with Cameron Diaz and Tim Russert *OR* Lucy Liu and Gandalf?

YOU MUST CHOOSE!

Would you rather have sex with...

Randy Quaid *OR* an Indian version of Viggo Mortensen?

A soft and gentle Ted Koppel *OR* a fast and furious Pillsbury Dough Boy?

A three way with J-Lo and Peter Jennings *OR* Shakira and the Hamburglar?

Things to consider: Robble, Robble

YOU MUST CHOOSE!

Would you rather...

have a prehensile penis

OR

a detachable scrotum (patent pending)?

Would you rather...

have your sexual partner suddenly transported to New Orleans upon your achieving climax

OR

have your sexual exploits narrated and commented upon by the bodyless voices

of Al Michaels and John Madden?

Things to consider: one night stands, spite sex, Michaels and Madden's charming rapport

YOU MUST CHOOSE!

This or That?

Challenge yourself or your friends with the following quiz. Answers on page 165.

1. Famous Children's Book *OR* Nazi Nickname?
   - a. The Desert Fox
   - b. The Velveteen Rabbit
   - c. The Angel of Death
   - d. Super Fudge

2. NHL Team *OR* Historical Occurrence?
   - a. Colorado Avalanche
   - b. Missouri Compromise
   - c. Gadsden Purchase
   - d. St. Louis Blues

YOU MUST CHOOSE!

3a. Porn Star *OR* Meteorological Term?

    a. Summer Cummings

    b. Winter Solstice

    c. Jet Stream

    d. Busty Dusty

3b. Meteorologist *OR* Porn Term?

    a. Flip Spiceland

    b. Pearl Necklace

    c. Al Roker

YOU MUST CHOOSE!

4. Jessica Tandy Film *OR* Euphemism For Masturbation?

    a. Guarding Tess

    b. Choking The Chicken

    c. Driving Miss Daisy

    d. Polishing the Purple Army Helmet

5. Famous Indian Chieftain *OR* Euphemism for White Basketball Player?

    a. Sitting Bull

    b. Does-all-the-intangibles

    c. Shows-up-every-night

    d. Paula Poundstone

YOU MUST CHOOSE!

CHAPTER

3

NOT-QUITE-SUPER POWERS

Lucky you. The deity is in good spirits. Turns out, he was right all along. It is spelled "deity", not "diety." He's bubbling over with happiness, and wants to share it with you by bestowing upon you one of two peculiar, if not super, powers. Take your pick.

Would you rather...

be able to simulate the voice of anybody you meet

OR

simulate the hair?

Would you rather...

have the power to switch your emotions on and off

OR

be able to fully comprehend written material just by sniffing the words?

Things to consider: reading in the library/on subway, leadership potential

YOU MUST CHOOSE!

Would you rather...

have Bettie Davis eyes

OR

Charles Manson eyes?

YOU MUST CHOOSE!

Would you rather...

have a tape-dispensing mouth

OR

bottle opening nostrils?

Would you rather...

have Spanish subtitles appear as you speak

OR

have a photographic memory where all the people involved are replaced with the cast of *Night Court*?

Things to Consider: Bull

YOU MUST CHOOSE!

Would you rather...

be able to consume fatty foods without gaining weight

OR

be able to have unprotected sex without getting sexual diseases?

Things to consider: Syphilis, Chlamydia, hot fudge, gravy fries, cheese balls

YOU MUST CHOOSE!

Would you rather...

have taste buds all over your body

OR

have a malleable stress-ball head?

YOU MUST CHOOSE!

Would you rather...

have an ass-fax *OR* a Phillips head screwdriver outie belly button?

elastic lips *OR* reflective calves?

inflatable breasts *OR* adjustable palm lines?

Things to consider: messing with psychics

Would you rather...

be able to fast-forward life

OR

rewind it?

Things to consider: pelbin

YOU MUST CHOOSE!

Would you rather...

have the ability to talk clearly while dentists are working on your teeth

OR

permission to talk dirty?

YOU MUST CHOOSE!

Would you rather have your eulogy delivered by...

Jesse Jackson *OR* the guy who narrates all those movie trailers?

The ghost of Shakespeare *OR* Dr. Seuss?

Andrew Dice Clay *OR* Gallagher?

The Coa Coa Puffs bird *OR* the narrator to those old Snausages commercials?

YOU MUST CHOOSE!

The deity has decided he might want to take over the world (depending on his schedule). To aid him on his quest, he's decided to make you a supervillain.

Would you rather be...

The Laminator

OR

Dr. Humidity?

Would you rather be...

Rash Man (annoys foes with minor skin irritations)

OR

The Tenderizer (softens foes with rapid strikes of a mallet)?

YOU MUST CHOOSE!

Would you rather...

be able to fly but be afraid of heights

OR

be able to become invisible but be a compulsive masturbator?

YOU MUST CHOOSE!

Would you rather...

be able to increase the intensity/frequency of nearby throbbing objects

OR

be able to flatulate to the tune of "When the Saints Go Marching In"?

Would you rather...

have Gatorade saliva

OR

be able to murmur fluently in twelve languages?

YOU MUST CHOOSE!

Would you rather...

be able to insist on paying for the check but never actually get stuck with it

OR

know exactly what the person on the other end of the phone looks like simply by hearing their voice?

Would you rather...

be able to will your pot-belly to other parts of your body

OR

be first cousins with Ernest Borgnine?

Things to consider: this question excerpted from *Plato's Republic*

YOU MUST CHOOSE!

(Orthodox Jews only)

Would you rather..

have nice full flowing payois

OR

always know where the matzo is hidden?

YOU MUST CHOOSE!

Would you rather...

have a magic mirror that possesses Woody Allen's personality/sense of humor

OR

a coffee table that possesses the personality of ex-Pittsburgh Steeler, Franco Harris?

YOU MUST CHOOSE!

Good Parenting

These are the circumstances: The deity has decided to help you rear your child. You may question his technique-- after all, he's operating for reasons beyond your understanding.

Would you rather have the entertainment at your child's birthday party be...

Tony Robbins *OR* Richard Simmons?

Charles Bukowski *OR* Jerry Falwell?

50 Cent *OR* Betty Big Ones?

YOU MUST CHOOSE!

Would you lather...

(What began as a Japanese man's mispronunciation became an idea unto itself)

Would you lather... a hippopotamus?

Would you lather... John Sununu?

Would you lather... the Fry guys?

YOU MUST CHOOSE!

CHAPTER 4

COOL AND UNUSUAL PUNISHMENT

The deity is in a bad mood, and deities, as you may have read, tend to be just a tad wrathful. He's looking to vent his anger on one of his pet mortals, and his gaze happens to fall upon you. And so now you must suffer a horrible death, a violent torture, or something else horrific, disgusting, or just generally unpleasant. ☺

Would you rather...

melon-ball your left eye out

OR

drive two spikes into your kneecaps with a sledgehammer?

Would you rather...

slide naked down a fire man's pole covered with tacks into a pool of scotch

OR

cheese-grate the skin off your left forearm?

YOU MUST CHOOSE!

Would you rather...

rest your head on a tee and then get smacked with the full-speed swing of Mark McGwire

OR

have a bowling ball dropped from twenty feet onto your groin?

YOU MUST CHOOSE!

Would you rather be stuck on a stalled bus with...

coked up Hollywood types *OR* obese Hare Krishnas?

incontinent Labradors *OR* the paparazzi?

forlorn albinos *OR* nosy pirates?

manic-depressive nuns *OR* autistic rodeo clowns?

condescending cobblers *OR* sullen blacksmiths ?

articulate half-orcs *OR* dizzy Erin Grey clones?

YOU MUST CHOOSE!

Would you rather have your cell phone ring function set on...

Airhorn OR Taser?

Throb OR Vacuum?

First Degree Burn OR Anti-Semitic Remark?

Faint OR Vietnam War Flashback?

Itch OR Ooze?

Wet Hacking Cough OR Surly Frenchman?

Tale of Tragic Irish Upbringing OR Awful Ronald Reagan Impression?

YOU MUST CHOOSE!

Would you rather...

be extruded through a spaghetti machine

OR

be buried alive in a pit of Play-Doh?

Would you rather...

dive head first off a 15 meter high-diving board into an empty pool

OR

drink a tall glass of liquid nitrogen?

YOU MUST CHOOSE!

Would you rather...

blend your foot and imbibe the result

OR

castrate yourself with a toe-nail clipper?

Would you rather...

be pumped with water until you burst

OR

be dehydrated to death by a giant one of those infomercial beef-jerky-making machines?

YOU MUST CHOOSE!

The deity has imprisoned you in a closed room. You are in a fight to the death. All enemies are hostile.

Would you rather fight...

100 toddlers OR 15 geese?

3 possessed lawnmowers OR the cast of *Dawson's Creek*?

1 vicious werewolf OR 6 bashful vampires?

extremely sleepy ninjas OR post-diet sumo wrestlers?

a real life incarnation of every team nickname of the NFC OR AFC?

a thousand evil pies OR a high school marching band?

YOU MUST CHOOSE!

Would you rather...

have your lips drawn and quartered

OR

have each of your fingers bent back until they snapped?

YOU MUST CHOOSE!

(For *Star Trek* nerds only)

Would you rather...

room with the evil Captain Kirk from *Episode 27*

OR

have sex with a Mugatu beast from *Episode 45*?

YOU MUST CHOOSE!

Would you rather...

have Wesley Snipes catch you picking your nose

OR

fall down in front of Pat Morita?

YOU MUST CHOOSE!

Would you rather...

administer Tabasco sauce eye drops

OR

rub a steak knife against your gums?

Would you rather...

sleep a night on a bed of peanut butter

OR

next to a humidifier full of urine?

YOU MUST CHOOSE!

Would you rather...

take a power drill in the Adam's apple

OR

fill your pants with raw meat and kick a pit bull in the side?

YOU MUST CHOOSE!

Would you rather....

spontaneously combust

OR

spontaneously turn into Harriet Beecher Stowe?

YOU MUST CHOOSE!

Grody to the Maximum Degree:
Would you rather...

have just eaten rice only to find out they were maggots

OR

be sucking on a endless succulent strand of spaghetti only to find out it's the umbilical cord of a woman who's just given birth?

Would you rather...

be caught masturbating by your grandmother

OR

vice-versa?

YOU MUST CHOOSE!

Would you rather...

smoke 100 cigarettes nasally

OR

tongue clean 10 blocks worth of New York City public phone mouth pieces?

Would you rather...

stick your tongue in an electric pencil sharpener

OR

have an ant crawl up your urethra Franklin and lay hundreds of eggs?

YOU MUST CHOOSE!

Would you rather...

relax in a Jacuzzi of a stranger's saliva

OR

have diarrhea in a gravity free chamber?

YOU MUST CHOOSE!

C H A P 5 T E R

WOULD YOU RATHER LIVE IN A WORLD WHERE...

The world is a funny place... But not funny enough. The deity is looking to spice it up and he's hired you as a consultant. First task: come up with a better introduction to this chapter.

Would you rather live in a world...

where Teletubbies were a common species of creature that lived in the wild

OR

where there were evil "Bizarro" arch-enemy versions of ourselves?

Things to consider: hunting

YOU MUST CHOOSE!

Would you rather live in a world...

where the convention of singing "Happy Birthday" was replaced with "You Ain't Seen Nothin' Yet" by Bachman Turner Overdrive

OR

where congressional debate was settled by dodgeball contests?

YOU MUST CHOOSE!

77

Would you rather live in a world...

where marijuana was legal

OR

where referring to yourself in the third person was illegal?

YOU MUST CHOOSE!

Would you rather live in...

the Star Wars Universe *OR* Shakespeare's England?

a Jane Austen Novel *OR* the neighborhood with the *Fat Albert* gang?

Biblical Egypt *OR* the world of Atari's *Centipede*?

Would you rather live in...

Kaiser-ruled Germany *OR* Pre-Dorothian *Oz*?

Colonial Williamsburg *OR* the recreated Colonial Williamsburg?

Tsarist Russia *OR* Czarist Russia?

YOU MUST CHOOSE!

Would you rather live in a world...

where genitals tasted like candy

OR

where a drum set appears at the moment of orgasm so that you may better express your ecstasy?

YOU MUST CHOOSE!

Would you rather live in a world...

where there was no such thing as pain, but also no such thing as sports

OR

where there was no such thing as world hunger, but also no such thing as Jim J. Bullock?

YOU MUST CHOOSE!

Would you rather live in a world...

where women were given equal pay, opportunity, and access to jobs

OR

where men experience the pains of the birth process along with women?

YOU MUST CHOOSE!

Would you rather live in a world comprised entirely of...

Nerf *OR* Tootsie roll?

flannel *OR* wicker?

ice-cream *OR* Alan Alda?

Would you rather live in a world painted by...

Van Gogh *OR* Seurat?

Rembrandt *OR* a six year old?

Monet *OR* Manet?

Bosch *OR* Boesch?

YOU MUST CHOOSE!

You are stranded on a desert island.

Would you rather have...

a bottle of Scope mouthwash *OR* a bottle of Jack Daniels?

a manicurist *OR* a donkey?

a slice of veal roast *OR* a poster of the 1984 Houston Rockets?

a box of Grapenuts, a wrench, and a pair of fuzzy dice *OR* a jar of Vaseline, a fake moustache, and a photograph of Spiro Agnew?

YOU MUST CHOOSE!

Would you rather live in a world...

where there was a rapper-like East Coast/West Coast feud of mimes

OR

where the pledge of allegiance was changed to the lyrics to "Eye of the Tiger"?

YOU MUST CHOOSE!

Would you rather live in a world without...

skin moisturizer *OR* cream cheese?

Sinbad *OR* Eskimos?

Men Without Hats' "Safety Dance" *OR* salmon?

David Copperfield *OR* oatmeal?

YOU MUST CHOOSE!

Workin' for the Man:

The deity has just finished a hostile take-over of your work place and he's changing the place up a bit. Schooled in the art of effective management, he's seeking employee input.

Would you rather work at a company where...

you are given great health benefits

OR

Thursday is "No Pants" day?

YOU MUST CHOOSE!

Would you rather work at a company where...

the dress code is prom wear from the 1970's

OR

your boss conveys your end-of-the-year evaluation through rap?

YOU MUST CHOOSE!

Would you rather be...

a crash test dummy *OR* a fluffer for animal nature documentaries?

the world's greatest rhythm gymnast *OR* the last man off the bench for the LA Clippers?

a Lionel Richie impersonator *OR* a Hobbit pimp?

a matador with a club foot *OR* a librarian with problem flatulence?
Or the reverse?

YOU MUST CHOOSE!

89

Would you rather...

have your therapist be James Taylor *OR* Bob Costas?

have your Lamaze coach be Marv Albert *OR* the guy from *Police Academy* who made all those crazy sound effects?

your blacksmith be Dan Rather *OR* John Stamos?

YOU MUST CHOOSE!

Would you rather... for beginners:

Would you rather...

be suave and sophisticated with nice hair

OR

rotund and misshapen with rickets?

Would you rather...

have $200

OR

$45?

Would you rather...

learn the teachings of Jesus

OR

those of Timothy Busfield?

YOU MUST CHOOSE!

The Would you rather...? Menu
Would you rather eat...

200 slices of American cheese *OR* 2000 raisins?

a cube of dry ice *OR* your own left foot?

every object in the dictionary between "flock" and "full" *OR* between "blimp" and "brown"?

the contents of a full vacuum cleaner bag *OR* forty-five dollars in nickels?

Would you rather eat...

a bowl of bat guano *OR* a mug of hot tea prepared with a used tampon?

14 full sticks of butter *OR* the contents of Michael Jackson's face?

all food in liquid form *OR* gaseous form?

Salmon Sorbet *OR* Dirty Coins and Cream?

Baked penguin *OR* Creamed Estrada?

YOU MUST CHOOSE!

Would you rather drink...

a Beefbrawler (gin, orange juice, ground beef, two shakers of salt sucked through a green onion)

OR

a Bloody Pilgrim (Kool-Aid, heavy cream and mushrooms pureed, topped with warm fat freshly liposucked from Elizabeth Taylor's thigh and upper arm)?

Would you rather eat...

The Emperor (2 pounds of roast beef sautéed in Roger Ebert's sweat consumed to the tune of "Ride of the Valkyrie")

OR

The Regent (2 charcoal briquettes on toasted role, eaten in the presence of 5 surly sailors)?

YOU MUST CHOOSE!

CHAPTER 7

WISHFUL THINKING

The deity has assumed corporeal form. He wears a white suit and is flanked by a miniature Latino man, also wearing a white suit. A plane is heard overhead, exciting the small man to announce its arrival. Twice. This could mean only one thing. You have arrived on Fantasy Island. Not only do you have the chance to fulfill a fantasy, but you get to choose between two.

Would you rather...

have a lake named after you

OR

have a popular children's multivitamin shaped in your image?

YOU MUST CHOOSE!

Would you rather...

bring in da' noise

OR

bring in da' funk?

Would you rather see...

Barry White chant the haftorah portion at a Bar-Mitzvah

OR

Al Gore do def comedy?

YOU MUST CHOOSE!

Would you rather live in a world...

have a mini-golf course lawn

OR

an air hockey dinner table?

Things to consider: Passing the salt

YOU MUST CHOOSE!

Would you rather...

be on a reality show

OR

punch everyone who has been?

Would you rather...

see Lincoln and Washington debate

OR

see them play a game of one-on-one basketball?

YOU MUST CHOOSE!

Would you rather interview...

Bill Clinton *OR* Prince?

Dick Gephart *OR* Dominique Wilkins?

J.D. Salinger *OR* J.D. Hogg

Jesus *OR* Tom Kite?

YOU MUST CHOOSE!

Would you rather...

touch the Pope

OR

meet Bill Bellamy?

YOU MUST CHOOSE!

Would you rather spend a day with...

El DeBarge *OR* George Bernard Shaw?

Ralph Sampson *OR* Ralph Nader?

Rommel and Charles Schultz *OR* Willie Nelson and Kubla Khan?

The founding fathers *OR* the casts of *The Cannonball Run 1* and *2*?

YOU MUST CHOOSE!

Would you rather have...

Wilt Chamberlin's basketball history

OR

his sexual history?

Would you rather split a bottle of whiskey with...

Jimmy "Super Fly" Snuka *OR* Andy Rooney?

Wilfred Brimley *OR* Webster?

Hunter S. Thompson *OR* Manute Bol?

YOU MUST CHOOSE!

If you could were a fly on the wall, would you rather reside...

on Tom Cruise's wall *OR* on Robin Williams's?

on porn queen Jenna Jameson's wall *OR* on *Dungeons and Dragons* creator Gary Gygax's?

on Tone Loc's wall *OR* Anne Maxson's?

YOU MUST CHOOSE!

Would you rather...

lasso Gabe Kaplan

OR

set up a volleyball net for Helen Hunt?

YOU MUST CHOOSE!

Fun With Spell-check

Sometimes Microsoft Word's spell-check can be a life-saver. Other times...

Word not in dictionary	-	Spell-check's suggestion
Chewbacca	-	chewable
Fartbeat	-	ferryboat
Beefball	-	befall
Buttball	-	butyl, biteable
Fillmore	-	filmier, filmgoer
briss	-	RBI's
McCheese	-	machete
dickwad	-	duckweed
Yankovic	-	no suggestions

YOU MUST CHOOSE!

The names of various famous people that have appeared in drafts of this book have been replaced with the spell-check's suggestions. Try to figure out the actual names. Answers on page 166.

Suggested words- famous person

1. Cyanide Pauper - ?

2. Simian Believer - ?

3. Fabliau, phobia, FBI - ? (clue: Italian superhunk)

4. Jason Boatmen - ?

5. Lays Milan - ?

6. Elite Gourd - ?

7. Cedar, Pig - ?

YOU MUST CHOOSE!

CHAPTER 8

PLAY BALL

Professional sports are in trouble. Free agency has obliterated team loyalty, good sportsmanship is a thing of the past, and the game is so much about the dollar that fantasy leagues now have fans fantasizing they are owners, competing with each other to make the most money. Something needs to be done about the sorry state of sports. Enter the deity (and you.)

You have just been hired by the head of the PGA to change one rule.

Would you rather...

allow loud heckling at greens

OR

require golfers to tee off of their caddy's crotch?

YOU MUST CHOOSE!

You have just been chosen to help pick one rule to make soccer more exciting.

Would you rather...

have grazing livestock scattered throughout the field

OR

if a goal is not scored in a game, have all players summarily executed?

YOU MUST CHOOSE!

As NBA commissioner,

Would you rather institute...

a 2 second shot clock

OR

a 3 feet tall maximum height rule?

YOU MUST CHOOSE!

You have been appointed baseball commissioner.

Would you rather...

put spikes on the outfield wall at baseball games

OR

light the infield on fire?

Would you rather...

if a player balks, he is shot on sight

OR

if a fan catches a foul ball, that fan gets to "do it" with that player's wife?

Things to consider: That last joke might be from old Letterman. We can't even remember.

YOU MUST CHOOSE!

113

You have just become boxing commissioner.

Would you rather...

limit punching to below the belt

OR

require whoopie cushion-like devices to be placed in gloves?

YOU MUST CHOOSE!

Mixed Blessings

"You take the good, you take the bad, you take them both and there you have the facts of life, the facts of life..." – Walt Whitman

Would you rather...

be able to jump like Dr. J. in the ABA but always have to wear those short shorts he had

OR

have the eloquence of Thomas Jefferson but have to wear colonial garb and wig?

YOU MUST CHOOSE!

Would you rather...

have the mind of William Shakespeare but the body of William Taft

OR

the mind of Albert Einstein but the body of Fat Albert?

Things to Consider: Possible "Fat Einstein" Cartoon

YOU MUST CHOOSE!

Would you rather...

be a brilliant essayist but have to wear a matching set of wristbands and headband at all times

OR

have heightened Stratego intuition, but talk like Liberace when asked to repeat yourself?

Would you rather...

look respectable in sweat pants but articulate all your thoughts aloud

OR

have a great short game in golf, but compulsively fondle yourself when the doorbell rings?

Things to consider: cocktail parties, making business deals

YOU MUST CHOOSE!

Would you rather...

have the courage of a lion but the ass of a baboon

OR

the wisdom of an owl but the head of Epstein from *Welcome Back, Kotter*?

Would you rather...

have a firm handshake but be severely lactose intolerant

OR

be loved by animals but require the signature of Cheech Marin for all your legal documents?

YOU MUST CHOOSE!

Sins

Sometimes circumstance makes a man do evil things. Other times the deity does. Why? That's right, reasons beyond your understanding. In any case, you must commit a horrible, terrible sin. You must turn, shall we say, the lesser of two evils.

Would you rather...

burn down an orphanage (resulting in only minor injuries)

OR

run over a litter of kittens with your lawn mower?

Would you rather...

kick your aunt in the stomach

OR

drop 200 turtles off a 40 story building?

YOU MUST CHOOSE!

Immoral Dilemmas

You are walking down the street and see an open briefcase with $1,000 in it. Across the street there is a police station. Do you spend the money on whores or crack?

Your boss, female, attractive, and married has insinuated that pleasuring her sexually will result in the advancement of your career. Do you partake in oral or anal sex?

You're driving at night and hit a dog. No one witnesses you hitting the dog. Do you broil or bake it?

You're waiting at a red light at 4 AM. There isn't a car in sight. No one would see if you ran the light. Do you masturbate with your left or right hand?

An old dirty vagrant with lip sores is pulled from the water and needs mouth-to-mouth resuscitation, which you know how to do. Do you partake in oral or anal sex?

YOU MUST CHOOSE!

CHAPTER 9

WOULD YOU...

The deity wants to see how desperate a mortal you are. How pathetic. How small. You will be quashed, the world shall be burned away in a fiery inferno, and the winds of time shall sweep away its charred remains, and we will create the world anew in our own image.... EVERLASTING!!!... uh... We mean says the deity. Anyway...

Would you ... punch your grandmother, not full-force, but solidly in the back of the neck for $16,500?

Would you... want to be immune from all traffic laws if you had to drive a 70's style van with a moonscape and Pegasus airbrushed on the side?

Would you... share an apartment with Corey Feldman to lower your rent by $600 a month?

YOU MUST CHOOSE!

Would you... permanently chain a penguin to your leg to be able to have sex with anyone you want?

Would you... wear your hair in a mullet for a month for $1200? (for women, $3900?)

Would you... cuddle with Boris Yeltzin to get your own sitcom with Justine Bateman? Vice-Versa?

YOU MUST CHOOSE!

123

Would you... invent a machine that sped technology but caused 1,000 deaths per year?

Things to consider: would you invent the car?

Would you... invent a machine that caused 1,000 hand injuries per year and killed one dumb person?

Things to consider: would you invent the blender?

Would you... invent a machine that worsened the hair of thousands of ignorant people and killed one unbelievably stupid and perverted person?

Things to consider: would you invent the crimper?

YOU MUST CHOOSE!

"The Million Dollar Man" Ted Dibiase once said that every man has his price, and the Deity's about to find out yours. He's making you an offer you can't refuse...or can you? If you can refuse the offer, name your price.

Would you... eat a tennis ball for $1,000?

Would you... spend two weeks in nothing but a g-string for $2,000?

Would you... sleep with your significant other's best friend for $10,000? What if that friend were "Handsome" Harley Race?

Would you... gain 150 pounds for $10,000?

Would you... eat human flesh for $1,000? $50,000?

Would you... for $38,000, get a seven minute lap dance from your grandmother dressed in nothing but a thong and prescription orthopedic shoes?

YOU MUST CHOOSE!

Would you... (if male) give up an inch of your height for an inch of penis size? If female, would you trade one inch of your significant other's height for an inch added to his penis size? How many inches would you trade?

Would you... run full speed into a brick wall for a life-size wax sculpture of Nipsey Russell?

Would you... give up socks if France promised to change its name to Funkytown?

YOU MUST CHOOSE!

Would you... like to be a member of the Libertarian party?

Would you... compliment Jimmy Carter's presidency for an egg sandwich and medium coffee?

Would you... want the artistic talents of Picasso if you could only paint guys named Cyrus?

YOU MUST CHOOSE!

Best of *Would You Rather* 1: Illustrated

Would you rather...

Be hole-punched to death

OR

Be eaten alive by the cast of Diff'rent Strokes?

YOU MUST CHOOSE!

Would you rather...
OR
©Justin Heimberg &David Gomberg
Wouldyourather.com

Have a ketchup-dispensing navel

a pencil-sharpening nostril?

YOU MUST CHOOSE!

Would you rather...

Have the head of Herve Villechaize (Fantasy Island's Tattoo) in place of your left hand and the head of Ricardo Montalban (Fantasy Island's Mr. Rourke) in place of your right hand

OR

be unable to go places without an entourage of bickering Vietnamese politicians?

YOU MUST CHOOSE!

133

Getting Personal

It's your turn to play deity. Challenge your friends with these personalized quandaries.

Would you rather...

share an eighteen hour car ride with (insert annoying acquaintance)

OR

put on (insert friend)'s socks every day for a month?

Would you...

have sex with (insert someone repulsive) to have sex with (insert someone desirable)?

YOU MUST CHOOSE!

Would you rather...

bathe and powder (insert disgusting acquaintance) twice a day every day for a week?

OR

slap a full nelson on (insert friend's mother) for five minutes?

YOU MUST CHOOSE!

Would you rather...

see (insert attractive acquaintance) naked

OR

see (someone you hate) wounded?

Would you rather...

take a tour of Vermont's covered bridges with (insert famous dictator)

OR

play Connect Four with (insert famous artist)?

YOU MUST CHOOSE!

CHAPTER 10

THE DEITY'S GREATEST HITS: VOLUME II: ELECTRIC BOOGALOO

The deity's been sniffing glue again. He's on random play again, and there's no telling what kind of dilemma may show up.

Would you rather...

walk like an eighty year old

OR

a two year old?

YOU MUST CHOOSE!

Would you rather...

have confederate flag irises *OR* Velcro body hair?

erasers for lips *OR* corkscrews for pinky fingernails?

mayonnaise tears *OR* Koolaid sweat?

YOU MUST CHOOSE!

Would you rather...

have breast implants made of sculpting clay *OR* cedar shavings?

Legos *OR* hydrogen?

bleu cheese *OR* live crickets?

glow-in-the-dark silly putty *OR* rice?

dark matter *OR* the soul of Terrance Trent D'Arby?

YOU MUST CHOOSE!

Would you rather...

turn into Sammy Davis Jr. when masturbating

OR

have the AOL "you've got mail" guy announce your ejaculations?

YOU MUST CHOOSE!

The deity has imprisoned you in a closed room. You are in a fight to the death. All enemies are hostile.

Would you rather fight...

a tiger with no front legs *OR* 800 bullfrogs?

3000 butterflies *OR* 1 bobcat?

Lawrence Taylor *OR* the cast of the *Wonder Years*?

10 Phil Donahues *OR* 3 Chuck Norrises?

300 remote control cars *OR* 30 sentient red rubber playground balls?

YOU MUST CHOOSE!

Would you rather...

emit steam from your ears when you're angry

OR

exude Tang from your hands when you're tardy?

YOU MUST CHOOSE!

Would you have sex with...

a bearded Paris Hilton *OR* a breaded Christina Applegate?

Glenn Close *OR* a three-times-the-normal-density Catherine Zeta Jones?

Rebecca Lobo *OR* an eight month pregnant Elizabeth Hurley?

the sublime Lynn Redgrave *OR* the subliming Vicki Lawrence?

YOU MUST CHOOSE!

Would you rather...

have a reverse digestive tract

OR

conduct all written work in the voice of Snoop Doggy Dogg?

Would you rather...

menstruate Yoo-Hoo

OR

have hot fudge post-nasal drip?

Things to consider: weight gain

YOU MUST CHOOSE!

Would you rather...

be only able to see yourself through Ernest Hemingway's eyes

OR

have self-esteem dependent upon your proximity to granite quarries?

Things to consider: Hemmingway's strict demands for machismo, quarry groupies

Would you rather...

have the ability to silence with a stare

OR

goose with a wink?

YOU MUST CHOOSE!

Would you rather...

have a head that reflects light like a disco party ball

OR

puff up like a blowfish when you sense danger?

YOU MUST CHOOSE!

Would you rather...

be unable to understand the written word unless read to you by *Dukes of Hazzard* star Tom Wopat

OR

have your legal name changed to "Doo-Doo McGee"?

Things to consider: office staff meetings, contract signings

Would you rather...

be able to communicate with animals, but only the nerds

OR

imbibe knowledge through a sweet sherbet?

YOU MUST CHOOSE!

Would you rather..

have the peripheral vision of Magic Johnson

OR

the magic vision of Peripheral Johnson? (work in progress)

YOU MUST CHOOSE!

Would you rather...

have to communicate solely in baby talk

OR

in *Three's Company* style double entendre?

YOU MUST CHOOSE!

Would you rather...

have a toilet that bucked like a bronco

OR

a bigoted toaster oven?

Would you rather...

be incapable of closing your eyes at the same time

OR

have three children, all named Marshall?

YOU MUST CHOOSE!

Extra Credit: (Left-overs)

Would you rather...

have to wear clothes of airplane fabric clothing, have four knuckle fingers, pronounce every third word "kelbor", be allergic to Don Mattingly, and have a breeze that perpetually blows by making your hair look healthy and manageable like models'

OR

have to play all sports holding hands with Gil Gerard, speak like an 18th century British dowager, be shrouded in fog, age to 40 then reverse, and always feel like you do when you bite into an ice-cold popsicle with your most sensitive teeth?

YOU MUST CHOOSE!

Would you rather...

have your eyes always moving as if watching a ping-pong match

OR

be limited to cleansing yourself by use of a Dust Buster?

YOU MUST CHOOSE!

Would you rather...

have nipples that roved and wandered all over your body

OR

have hair that changes color and falls out in the autumn?

YOU MUST CHOOSE!

Would you rather...

see the world in Atari 2600 graphic quality

OR

in the perspective and outlook of the most jaded Hollywood agent in America?

Would your rather...

have mood lips (change color according to your mood)

OR

make the sound of the shaking of Boggle letter cubes when laughing?

YOU MUST CHOOSE!

Would you rather...

walk like an Egyptian

OR

date a girl with an unwavering propensity to party all the time?

YOU MUST CHOOSE!

Would you rather never be able to use...

toilet paper *OR* the letter "e"?

shampoo *OR* profanity?

shoes *OR* any verb other than "destroy"?

YOU MUST CHOOSE!

Would you rather...

be the Supreme Court Justices' sex slave for a day

OR

be wagon-trained by a pack of Oompa-loompas?

Would you rather...

vomit dice

OR

excrete *Monopoly* real estate?

YOU MUST CHOOSE!

Would you rather...

breath to rhythm to "Eine Kleine Nacht Musik" by Mozart

OR

have your first born look like Harold Ramis?

Would you rather...

be able to hear every cell phone ring in your neighborhood

OR

smell every fart?

YOU MUST CHOOSE!

Would you rather...

have a harmonica implanted in your nasal passageway

OR

have all your memories eventually fade into the tone of rap videos?

Would you rather...

urinate crazy string

OR

lactate grits?

YOU MUST CHOOSE!

Would you rather...

have your face on the national currency

OR

your ass on the national currency?

Would you rather...

have sex in front of your grandparents

OR

the *American Idol* judges?

YOU MUST CHOOSE!

Would you rather...

experience a brain freeze (literally) **OR** heart break (literally)?

have porcelain skin (literally) **OR** hair of gold (literally)?

have the eye of the tiger (literally) **OR** broccoli pubic hair (literally)?

YOU MUST CHOOSE!

For thirty seconds, would you rather...

lie down naked on a Benihana table

OR

have your mouth stretched around the part of a lawnmower where the grass spits out while it mows high grass?

YOU MUST CHOOSE!

Would you rather have your dreams written and directed by...

Quentin Tarantino OR Woody Allen?

Ed Wood OR the creators of the OC?

Spike Lee OR Stan Lee?

John Hughes OR Ron Jeremy?

Would you rather...

drool Drain-O

OR

exhale Raid?

YOU MUST CHOOSE!

Answer Key

Answers to This or That?

1) **a.** NHL **b.** H.O. **c.** H.O. **d.** NHL

2) **a.** nazi (Rommel) **b.** book **c.** nazi (Mengele) **d.** book

3a) **a.** porn star **b.** weather term **c.** weather term **d.** porn star

3b) **a.** meteorologist **b.** porn term **c.** both

4) **a.** Tandy film **b.** euphemism **c.** Tandy film **d.** euphemism

5) **a.** chieftain **b.** euphemism **c.** euphemism **d.** neither

Answers to Spell Check Quiz

1. Cyanide Pauper – Cyndi Lauper
2. Simian Believer – Simon Bolivar
3. Fabliau, phobia, FBI - Fabio
4. Jason Boatmen – Jason Bateman
5. Lays Milan – Alyssa Milano
6. Elite Gourd – Eliot Gould
7. Cedar, Pig – Pia Zadora

Answers to Mystery Quiz

1. Austin
2. 2.5
3. Millard Fillmore, Dennis Johnson, and fifteen pounds of ham
4. **a.** Frank Sinatra **b.** the pancreas **c.** not applicable
5. "Break My Stride" by Matthew Wilder

Additional *Would You Rather...?*
questions and products are available at
wouldyourather.com.

- Board Games
- Calendars
- Clothes
- Busts of the Authors
- More Comedy
- Publicity Info
- Bulk Quantity Discounts
- And more!!!!!!

From the authors of *Would You Rather...?* comes another collection of over three hundred absu
alternatives and deranged dilemmas. Filled with wacky wit, irreverent humor, and twisted pop-cultu
references, *Would You Rather...? 2: Electric Boogaloo* asks you to ponder questions such as:

WOULD YOU RATHER...

be a Siamese twin
connected at the lips

OR

at the soles of your feet?

have your hostage
negotiator be Dick Vitale

OR

Ike Turner?

have your cell phone
ring function set on "Taser"

OR

"Airhorn"?

www.wouldyourather.com

A FALLS MEDIA BOOK
Humor   **USA $9.95** / CAN $13.99